Brady Toliver's

Love, Triumph, and Defeat

Love, Triumph, and Defeat

Brady C. Toliver II
"Mr. Septillion"

© 2014 by Brady Toliver II

ISBN 978-1-893937-05-5

All Rights Reserved.
No part of this book may be reproduced, in any form, without the
written permission from the author, unless by a reviewer who wishes
to quote brief passages.

Printed in the United States
Independent Publishing Corporation
Chesterfield, MO USA

Table of Poems

1	Love
2	Breathe
3	The Drums Of Life
4	The March
5	Timing
6	Saturday Morning Flow
7	Digitize
8	Yoga Love
9	LTD
10	From Here To There
12	I Cubed
13	Risen
14	The Light
15	Left Or Right
16	Oh So Happy
18	Righteous Steps
19	Dumb Flow
20	Dumb Flow II
22	Universal State
23	Past The Void
24	Dear Presidents
26	Pain
28	Good Love Hunting
29	Wedding Bells
30	Listening
31	AC
32	Ode To The Life

34	IS
35	Hello
36	Navigation
37	Give And Take
38	Love Machine
39	Untitled I
40	Arrival
41	Wisdom
42	The Purge
43	Untitled II
44	Missed
45	Flying
46	Forever
47	The Soul
48	Marriage
49	The Balance
50	Full Moon
52	The Illusion
53	The Beat Of Life
54	Dreams
55	The Come Back

Acknowledgements

I want to thank the Creator of all things. I appreciate the journey. The part I've chosen and the part she has laid out for me. Special thanks to my molders. A.K.A., my parents, Brady and Cathy. I am truly humbled by all of the sacrifices you made for me to succeed. Of course thank you to all of the companies that presented me awards for my skillset and in turn fired me because of my passion. I still love y'all. Special shout out to all of my true friends. You all know I appreciate the unconditional love. Last but not least thank you to the women who showed me how to give and receive love even when I wasn't worthy. Namaste

Love

With so much pain being released during the holiday season I'm writing this to highlight the natural duality of life.
Be not attached to that which is impermanent.
Good looks, money, life, cars, marriage, etc…
Stay attached to the one thing that powers procreation.
LOVE?
Love.
Love!
When everything leaves you, the universe is making room for new and fresh energy called LOVE.
As always, peace and Love.

Breathe

Breathe!
Breathe as if this one led to the next one.
Breathe as if it might be your last one on earth and if it isn't do it again.
Breathe as if the love you want depended on the fullness of your breath.
Just breathe as if the trees and bushes needed all that you have to give.
Just remember it all starts with one breath.

The Drums Of Life

With a four count beat I ask you to circle up...
Kindred spirits, countrymen/women, aliens et al.
Gather round and listen as I shout your mind castle.
Celebrate TODAY because tomorrow may never be,
but TODAY is everything we can be, do, and have.
So shout it out.
So our parallel world will deliver it...
just for you to give to the next...
I hope the GOD in you hears the GOD in me.
Dance and sing with me so that our vibrations will change the
canvas of the matrix we embody.
Shake that body, sing, shout, two step, line dance.
Do whatever it takes to shake the fog.
Now that you are free...
Go be whatever it is you choose!

The March

2 4 6 8 marchin' to da cadence of life.
In step off rhythm.
In step off rhythm.
This one touches the left brain to help you solve the complexities of existence…
2 4 6 8 marchin' to the cadence of life.
In step off rhythm.
In step off rhythm…
Wait I thought 12 plus 4 equals 16.
Years of education
plus 2 yields master of the universe and a guaranteed retirement…
No guarantees, except we are guaranteed to give and take…
2 4 6 8 marching to da cadence of life.
In step off rhythm.
This one touches the right brain to help ease the pain.
Is it love you want?
cuzz its love you IS.
I AM YOU
cuzz it is U N I verse.
2 4 6 8 marchin' to da cadence of life.
In step off rhythm.
In step off of rhythm.

Timing

Let's get it started...
give me a boom bap, boom bap.
For the musically inclined that's a boom with cha mouth and a
clap with cha hands.
Ready? Here we go.
Boom bap, boom bap, boom bap.
Shout out to mother earth and father sky.
I can't lie.
Woke up this morning ascending off the bed with da help of
the higher powers.
Boom bap, boom bap, boom bap.
Just me, my soul, vision, and my yoga mat.
Yoga?
Mat?
Boom bap, boom bap, boom bap.
Yeah ya know positions to let my soul flow.
Open, close, oops don't lose control.
Deep breath in thru ya nose out thru ya mouth.
Nice and steady I knew y'all was ready.
Boom bap, boom bap, boom bap.
She was wearing red
I was in yellow.
She asked about orange
Um, why yes, Hit her with da greens.
She said I see you getting lean.
I looked in her eyes saw da blues.
Skies that is...
Together we landed in indigo for that sutra flow.
Boom bap, boom bap, boom bap.
Off to the white light wearing all black Cuzz I hit cha with Dat
boom bap!

Brady Toliver

Saturday Morning Flow

I go and go.
Rest when I must.
Sleep how I need.
Sex indeed.
Recycle the flow.
I go and go.
For the know, I shoot infinite wisdom indeed.
Sitting pretzel style.
Give and receive energy from the planet.
Eating to live or living to eat.
I choose life so gotta eat right.
Left brain dominant, Right brain enthusiast equals harmony.
I go and go.
Rest when I need.
Sleep how I need.
Sex indeed.
Recycle the flow.
I eat more greens hoping the SUN that gives them life Will
light the kundalini
Lifting me to a higher flow.
Slow, fast, up and down… Flow
Oops gotta GO.

Digitize

Laying digital truths for your cataracts.
Don't be fooled by the media.
This war is eternal.
Ying vs Yang.
Smoke.
Chaos,
Safety.
Magic.
You are not safe...
How does that feel?
Crazy enough to grab a gun?
1000 rounds of ammo.
Acting like a gazelle in a den full of lions.
Wake up.
We are all targets.
Welcome to da jungle.

Brady Toliver

Yoga Love

Yo ga.
Yo ga da love of my life.
Yo ga
y o ga da love of my life.
Da love of my life.
Girl da first day I hit da mat I knew you were the one.
Yo ga yo ga.
Da love of my life.
You are me and I'm you.
All you ask is that I try all da moves.
Nice and relaxed.
When I hit the spots you send waves of energy.
Nice
Da love of…
Now that the clouds are clear…
I can see the yogi in me.

LTD

I just wanted to write this to y'all.
A letter to my family.
Zimmerman, Martin, and Brown.
All my days as a kid I never knew what was real.
Mind shaped by my environment; West County,
North side,
Black Pride,
American King with a dark shade.
IN case you didn't know.
Thought I was like you.
According to the history books…
God the creator said we are all him.
So I knew from the beginning I'd be winning.
However, every time I look at the news It seems people like me
are losing.
Survival of da fittest, but this is America home of the brave land
of the free.
Why don't you understand me?
Put here by force.
Not my first choice now that I'm here.
Why do you fear?
Yes we are the same.
I cut…
You bleed from the vein.
Whether you or me it is God that we see.

Brady Toliver

From Here To There

Love, triumph, defeat.
Imagine the love you've never had.
Then it shows up.
Like wala magic.
Not magic.
you called for it.
Hello....
Baby, when you coming home?
Not sure, closing this deal.
Well I need you and your touch.
Something I can feel.
Damn it feels good to be wanted.
Too busy being hunter.
Pushin' love under, being boy wonder.

Love triumph defeat, Love triumph defeat, Love triumph
defeat.

Who knew love could be unique.
Finally made it home.
If she only knew why I work so hard.
Dreamin' of days between the sheets.
Explorin' all the things we practice in yoga.
Back to the grind, gotta get my shine.
Plaques, awards, money, and trips.
Phone rings again... Baby when ya...
Sweets we going to Europe.
She doesn't seem happy.
I ignore it cuzz the crown changes the frown.
At least that was my thought.

Love triumph defeat, Love triumph defeat, Love triumph
defeat.

Triumph is the eye of the beholder - makes love even bolder.
Phone rings…
Hello, my dude we need to rap.
What's good…
You know you my guy.
Yeah I know, you would never disrespect.
Well, ya lady… stop!
My heart just dropped.
Already knew before he even said it.
In my mind I already lost what I thought was mine.
Plenty of phish, eharmony, and match what da "fluck."
I was on my grind - wanted to show her more.
So off to the world I go.
Back from foreign lands, career on da rocks.
Da bet I made wasn't with da real.
IN da midst of defeat I still rise.
In the end, blaze your own trail so you can live to tell.
The story is real.
Love - Triumph - Defeat is so unique.

Brady Toliver

I Cubed

According to the scriptures I am who I say I am.
I cubed.
So let it flow.
I am creative.
I am a supreme lover.
I am a great family man.
I am lean and healthy.
I am a great business man.
I am the black Warren Buffet.
I am debt free.
ON bended knee I pray to thee.
Answer my prayers because I am YOU.
You are in me.
No one can separate what is family.

Love, Triumph, and Defeat

Risen

Rise above never resting in a tub.
Sorrow for tomorrow.
Blessed is the work.
Work is for the blessed.
Be careful of who you trust.
Your best friend will leave ya.
Open your heart.
He never left he only moved on to what's next for him.
Allowing you to have space for what is right for you.
Don't despise those that attack.
They are playing chess when life is a game of GO.
Sometimes you lose when you win and win when you lose.
In GO you choose your move.
Sometimes it is good to rest while the others flutter around in space.
Mark your spot and rest your vessel.
Your season will come to make your way.

Brady Toliver

The Light

In the midst of darkness you can see the light.
I forgot to get on my knees at night.
Busy worrying about what to do.
Man it is easy to forget the GOD in you.
Prayer, meditation, be still.
If you ever think God ain't real -
lay on your back in a field and look up at 1 million reasons to believe.
You may not know what to call him, but she will surely answer when you do.
For every one step you take she will go 100.
So why don't I meditate in you.
On you and about you.
Even when I forgot to pray I always remembered your way.

Left Or Right

Left or right?
This is like that game where everything is the same til you hit a certain level.
Next step you are on another board.
It looks kind of familiar but not really.
Choice is like a voice.
We all have it.
Whether it is a sign or box.
So Left of Right?
Been going to da right, might be time to check the left, so I can be right.
Man if I had a crystal ball…
Even though I don't,
I still stand tall y'all.
So don't fear da fall, summer, or spring, cuzz winter may bring your dreams true.
Sure as the sky is blue GOD loves you.

Oh So Happy

Stayed away not because I didn't want to be with you.
Was putting my time in.
Yeah da love was good and you put me thru some changes.
Like remember the time we spent the whole weekend just writing and making love.
Oh so happy we were Love, Love.
Oh so happy we were love, love.
The changes we made last a lifetime.
Gave up the weed replaced with da greens.
Kale, spinach, and arugula.
Hadn't seen my abs in a while, til I laid eyes on that smile.
It was a cool day in September.
God sent me a message.
Walked in to teach my class.
Yeah I saw that ass… ooops.
You sat in the front row I was nervous as hell.
Class was over and I walked over to say good day.
You said boy don't play.
Oh so happy we were Love, love.
Oh so happy we were love, love.
The changes we made last a lifetime.
You said I know who you are.
My girls told me about you.
They said you make 'em sweat.
Indeed.com I knew I was the bomb.
She said don't get da big head.
I said alright.
Asked for her number.
She said yeah right.
Oh so happy we were love, Love.
Oh so happy we were love, love.

The changes we made last a life time.
Met my crew at the bar and the music was jamming.
Hit da floor ready to sweat some more.
Turned to da left and guess who I saw?
Yeah ya know.
She was from da floor to da ceiling.
She gave me that feeling.
Grabbed her by da hips and we began to dip.
We got lost in da music, 7 years later 2 kids and a house, I'm glad I chose you as my spouse.

Brady Toliver

Righteous Steps

Righteous.
The root is right,
but being it causes friction.
Leading to addiction
to perceived facts.
Back to my emotion.
Leading to devotion to the illusion.
Leading to a contusion of the brain and heart.
Choose being righteous.
It starts when the bull creeps in.
Merging with the shit.
So what you get is somebody being right, giving up their life to
lay in the pit awaiting.
The piss and da moan.
Da shit and da foam.
I choose the righteous path so I can laugh in the face of the
replacement.
As long as your needs are being met No need to fret.
Catch me, Pret a Manger.
Stay on the move to avoid danger.
Do what's best so righteous steps are blessed to reduce the stress.

Dumb Flow

I stay fresh.
Baby powder is what she calls me.
And that's before I was deep.
Put her azz to sleep.
Woke up to da beat of da drum.
She thought it was a gun, but it was my frank in her tum.
Tummy that is.
She had my frank wrapped like a mummy ya dig.
Beef Frank Love

Brady Toliver

Dumb Flow II

Um tap um tap
Um dada um tap
Um dada um tap
Mesmerized by da juice.
Bought to get loose.
No dance floor, but we still grooving.
Dj got dem gurls steady moving.
Sistas been twerkin' for centuries.
Walking thru da club inhalin' da smoke.
Steady choking.
Brothers grabbing azz and whistling.
I'm just listening.
Trying to find my nitch.
Yeah to make my pitch.
Na, not a tent.
Rather a splint to save the lungs
Meanwhile pictures snappin', booties clappin' and ninjas
trickin'.
Liquor pourin'.
Still lookin' for my way.
I'm so chill they never imagined.
I'm da bro that net like Jigga.
Not because I slang drugs.
No, not me, but because I save and I slave for myself and my
team.
Follow my dream.
Back to the commotion
Sistas is confused.
White gurls abused.
She tell fam that she loves the blunts and he can get it wet…
Gurl please… disease indeed.

You are more than weed, pills, and trappin'.
Listen to da trippy will leave ya tripped, stalled, fall, fallen.
Time stalling.
Peace to da queens that hold ya up.
Peace to da pank toes that hold ya down and support ya.
I wrote this so you know.... GROW

Brady Toliver

Universal State

Universal state.
Born September 25, 1978.
On time definitely not late.
Tad bit early but still expected.
Came out feet first.
Nurses looked and said, look at his feet.
Feet grew and matched my age til I was 14.
Moms would always say you got places to go.
Ma'ma you was right.
So let's get right to it.

Past The Void

Love, triumph, and defeat.
Light meets dark.
Darkness runs.
Open to change of seasons.
Darkness retreats only to rise from defeat.
Behold, the giver of life never needs a knife.
Love is the cutter and the healer.
Triumph is victory's creation.
Yes, sort of like masturbation.
Better yet, incubation.
Tri umph c a n be short and sweet.
We pray for long and neat.
Just like the Nasdaq we don't welcome a pause.
No one wants to be caught with their pants down.
Defeat doesn't care.
He comes in the broad day light.
Just when we are standing to raise our hand.

Dear Presents

War is heaven sent.
Civil war that is.
There is an old saying.
Take care of your backyard before you go clean another. War between brothers is unlike another.
Blue vs Gray.
Gray vs Blue an outsider is bound to lose (Chorus)

Allow the people of the world to decide their fate.
If we spend too much time, it will be too late for US.
Our kids will miss the bus.
We are already behind the most developed countries when it comes to education.
The money you are willing to spend on war…
Spend it on our youth

Take care of your backyard before you go clean another. War between brothers is unlike another.
Blue vs Gray.
Gray vs Blue an outsider is bound to lose (Chorus)

They deserve the truth.
The truth about life and the world.
Told from the aspect of a lil girl that lost her father in Vietnam.
All she had was the love of her mom.
Dad gone forever.
All because the president was clever.

Take care of your backyard before you go clean another. War between brothers is unlike another.
Blue vs Gray.
Gray vs Blue an outsider is bound to lose (Chorus)

War no more.
More war - the more we are torn.
Allow others to be reborn.
Look at the outcome of our civil war.
We started off on a different path.
Our job is not to dictate others fate.
We need to tend to our land, before our fate is out of our hands.
Bands will make her dance, but bombs will kill their moms.
And dads and the kids will kill our paths.
Bombs strapped to backs.
Let go in the middle of packs.
Of people.
War… there is no equal.

Brady Toliver

Pain

The pain is so deep.
Enough to wake the sleeping.
Man how do I keep up?
Gave up the chronic so I face the pain.
Didn't know how it affects da brain.
Gotta figure out a way to use my emotions.
To part the oceans of people and show them how to thrive not
just survive.
I feel your pain and am one with you

When you cry I cry
When you're hungry I crave
When you are lonely I sigh

I want you to know it is ok to cry.
And sometimes want to die.
Pick yourself up and know these feelings come and go.
Pack your bags and off to the world you go.
Did you ever think it would be this way?
Yes or no, no or yes.
Doesn't matter.
It is just chatter.
Block it out.
The outside world, your girl, or guy, and family.

When you cry I cry
When you are hungry I crave
When you are lonely I sigh

Love, Triumph, and Defeat

If it seems like it is too much...
The heat is on and bills are coming due.
Come out of the shade and realize on the other side the universe
has a glass of lemonade.
So don't delay go out and play.
Just remember do it your way.
No matter what they say.
Because at the end of the day it is U N I verse.

Brady Toliver

Good Love Hunting

Running for love.
We use to run from love.
All she wanted me to say was I love you today.
Pain from the past was like a dam.
Hoover that is.
She jumped it, climbed, and crawled.
But couldn't withstand it all.
Yeah I pushed her away because I couldn't tell her I loved her today.

I never learned to love.
Only to fuck and control... Her mind and body.
I never learned to love only fuck and control her mind and body.

All of them.
Why couldn't I just have all of them?
Short, tall, fit to chubby.
I loved them all and they wanted a hubby.
Makin' them cum was enough for me.
At 34 I realize there is more in store.
Man I wished there was a book in the store.
That could have saved those feelings and emotions.

I never learned to love.
Only fuck and control... Her mind and body.

Afraid to say I love you back because How long would it last.
Parents never showed it, so how could I figure it out.
Doomed from the start.
Damn hearts surely part.
From the beginning to the end I've learned to love.
Not to be so vain and to express my pain.
Love only starts when you say it and show it.

Wedding Bells

Wedding after wedding I see what it means to wed thee.
Some do it for the right reasons.
Some do it out of spite.
In spite of being single.
Man that's a jingle.
Only if they knew the joy of union.
One should not rush into fusion.
Avoid the delusion.
Not for the kids.
Parents.
My mom wants a grand baby.
Then tell her to adopt.
Not drop pressure onto you.
This isn't a game full of redos or take backs.
Check the facts and the costs.
Make the wrong choice and you will be calling her boss.
Cashin' checks to keep your respect.
But when things go right it is live like dynamite.
Long and blissful.
No stress and not a chore.
More like a smooth dance on the floor.
Fred Astaire and his lady.

Listening

Had a great conversation with a sista that claimed to be a
radical on sabbatical.
Young man I have 30 years on you
Of not listening to those who tell you what to do.
Do you know they really don't want you to grow.
School is to socialize you to da norms.
Compartmentalize you like dorms.
To paralyze you with charms.
Some end up with bracelets because they couldn't face it.
Deseg programs to build more schools.
Yet they don't give you the tools to succeed.
Did you know that kid they call dumb is up at 4:30AM to
catch the bus to the burbs.
Yet his voice is unheard.
Plays on the ball team.
Yet his talent is losing steam.
Cuzz he gets home at quarter to 9.
Read books? No time.
Cuzz I'm up at a half past 4.
Yet the school system says give me some more.
Ship in da poor.
Ignore the schools that are near. Ship them away. Way out my
dear.
They will never know because the colored are slow.
The role of teacher is not to lie or pry. It is to teach how to
think.
Out side the box. What is a box?
We live in a circle.
GOD can't fit in a box and neither can I.
Think or die.
Why not try?

AC

I need an AC pimpin' when it gets hot.
Able Cheerleader to hold down the spot when I'm out pushing my lot.
Wasn't sure what I really wanted when it came to a mate or partner.
Some father's precious daughter.
Proper management is key.
Being a listener is ideal.
Being real trumps all.
Real love that is.
Realizing that it comes from within.
Believing you are the next of kin.
Kindred spirits made to ascend.
Bare the falls.
Withstand it all and laugh a lot.

Ode To The Life

On the phone with my mans today.
We was rappin' about the trials and tribulations of life.
How we both don't have a wife nor kids, but like Adam we
have a rib.

Life is like a merry go round that slows down four times a year
to hop on.
Whatcha' say now.
Break a leg, Peggy's dead.
Pop a beer.
Have no fear.
So you get that wife you were looking for and the kids you
must adore.
Your life, so grand indeed.
But your soul, you never feed.

You've lost 4 jobs throughout your career.
They call you a jumper as in John Deere.
This last go round they celebrated your success all while calling
you a mess.
The blessing was in the split, because they knew you were 2
legit to quit.
Universe had already sent you the message so it was no surprise.
They could see it in your eyes.

Life is like a merry go round that slowz down 4 times a year to hop on.
Whatcha' say now.
Break a leg Peggy's dead.
Pop a beer.
Have no fear.
So you get that wife you were looking for and the kids you must adore.
Your life, so grand indeed.
But your soul, you never feed.

So when you said give me 30 minutes and I'm out.
They thought you would scream and shout.
You almost forgot the plan…
The cost was paid.
So the boss been made.
To walk that fine line is your design and to spit these lines.
From the spirit, so all those can hear it.

Brady Toliver

IS

So it is what it is.
People been saying it for years.
Holding back my tears.
Scared to face my fears.
Yet they keep appearing.
God you have forced my move.
For SHE has a plan.
And it is within my reach.
For as long as I adhere to the path.
Beach, beach, beach.
I can relax by the waves.
She does save those that listen with a lil ambition.
Surely you can become if you are willing to run or crawl.
Climb that wall.
Embark on your soul's journey.
And work it will never be.
Oh the sites you will see.
Just remember dream the dream.
And do the things that are not foreseen.
And the dream will be there for all to see.

Hello

I've been sending you some messages.
Some you reply to - some you don't.
You never said that you won't or can't, so I won't rant.
Just say yes is your tagline.
So tag you're it.
An old fashion dude.
Opening the door is a must.
Pulling out the chair of course.
Flowers.
Your choice.
Love, I've had a few.
The things I will do to bring you around.
I'm sure he loves you and the love was there.
Time we must not spare.
I saw the look in your eyes.
You know the time I made you cry.
Tears of joy.
When the Dr. said it was a boy.
And a girl.
Oh what a world.
How far we've come.
For the times when we were young.

Navigation

Seems like the road is plenty.
Obstacles… a few.
Triumphs many.
But like the candy, it is all good and plenty.
Gotta get movin'.
Doing what I'm doing.
Educating the youth on how to get loose.
Stay away from the noose.
Educating the parents on how to reach their goals.
Without digging into debt like moles.
So to grow is to know.
To know is to search.
To search.
You'll go berserk.
To be berserk.
You put in work and stay alert.
Because one day it will all work.

Give And Take

I remember the first time.
Like it was the last time.
Walked into your office.
Set up my display.
You walked in and my heart said I wanna play.
Your partner was asking questions.
My neck was strechin'.
To see if you were just like me.
Single and ready to mingle.
You asked me a couple of questions then started to point.
I pictured us married and rolling a joint.
Makin' you love me.
I do declare.
Man I was trippin' cuzz your underwear was within my stare.
The outline I saw thru that sundress.
My day was made when I saw no ring.
I was so happy I started to sing.
What impressed me more was the information you store.
Between your shoulders.
After I left I caught my breath.
Couldn't wait to see you again.
Got to the car and called my boy.
Told him I found her.
He said again.
Lil did I know we were connected thru friends.
All I needed to know is would your love stand.
Crushed when I found out I knew your man.
Guess that's what happens when the good ones are few.

Brady Toliver

Love Machine

I love how you ignore me when I walk in.
That's ok cuzz I'm still go win.
Yo heart.
Da chart and all those that part.
On my mission ordained by the creator.
She said no one is greater.
If I stay on da elevator.
Top floor here I Is.
She broke off my rib.
Created you in her image.
So no way I could mismanage.
Love.
Not damage.
In da past yeah I would.
Steal your love with my hand mudras.
Got ya feigning.
For my member that's 8 and leaning.
Plus my taste buds add 4.
Surely my 12 you will adore.

Untitled I

To move forward sometimes you gotta side step.
Shake it off, then roll out.
To lead the people out of the forest…
Sometimes they need to know you have been there.
You know - where it is rough.
Where it is tough.
Like 07 08 09 10.
If they know you can go.
Go past the façade.
They know you are witty and gritty.
And you can dance thru the pain like Diddy.
Come back up and roll da dice.
Twice as nice.
They know you got muddy and will arrive.

Brady Toliver

Arrival

Dropped off her back in 78.
My mom said I came on time.
Slide out feet first.
The nurse damn near cursed.
Sayin, Ohhh lard, look at his feet.
My mom smiled and said so unique -
He's got places to go and people to see.
He was created to be… what the creator - wanted to see.
Yo, I'm here GOD, ready and willing to do the work.
Ready for my freedom.
I know freedom is not free.
So time I will give Like Adam gave his rib.
I'll make sure the people will hear me.
AS if they are standing near me.
From U to me.
Me as the medium to the people that be.
Like toys to tikes.
Jordan's to Nike.
Our lessons will be the blessings.

Wisdom

When you think you are at the bottom... the top isn't too far away.
When you feel on top... remember the bottom is the denominator.
Either way keep going.

Brady Toliver

The Purge

I hope this letter releases all my pain.
I pushed 'em to the brink.
I wanted thee…
To hear like ink and a voice box.
Instead they thought it was the 24th hour and a bomb dropped.
I swear I'm not Edward Snowden.
We was da dream team.
So it seemed.
Speakin' two different languages.
Spanish vs Swahili.
What da dealio?
No Bueno.
Played me like Uno.
I should have known like Juno.
The structure wasn't ready.
Stagnant like a pond.
Cuzz I flow like the ocean.
Devotion to motion.
My cause is Love.

Love, Triumph, and Defeat

Untitled II

Fall in love with yourself.
Pursue freedom.
Act today.

Brady Toliver

Missed

Fell for you and lost myself.
Guess that's what I get for putting you on a shelf.
So it is me that I see, even in a tree.
On bended knee I ask the Lord for thee.
The key to my soul.
Know I got control.

Flying

Only once the drugs are gone.
I know I'm flying.

The drugs could be food, shrooms or the alcohol we consume.
WAsn't until they left the room… that I knew I was doomed.
I wish I could fly, but they only made me feel like dying.

Only after the drugs were gone.
I knew I could fly.

Fly high above the sky.
We are new to this.
So it is hard to stay true to this.

Only once da drugs were gone.
I knew I'm flying.

From a whole apple pie to 4 blunts of that lye.
I felt I'm dying.
I felt I'm dying.
The drugs just wouldn't leave me alone.
Almost like I made a clone.
Who constantly lived in the danger zone.
The addiction was women.
I make them flying.
I make them flying… in the ecstasy of love.
In their womb I dominated with love.
I knew I'm flying.

Only once the drugs were gone.
I knew I'm flying.

Yoga was the savior.
Allowing me to see women as more than just a freak or whore.
But more someone to adore and build with.
Now we are flying.

Brady Toliver

Forever

If we lived forever?
How could we give praise?
On these finite days.
In these abstract ways.

The Soul

Woke up and my soul was crying.
She said my body been lying.
While my mind been grinding.
Eyes weren't watering because the vision been clear.
We had a problem with da steering.
So instead of hearing da cheers we focused on the boos.
So we switched shoes.
Slowed down the pace.
Looking in the mirror.
My face got clearer.
God I am and so are you.
All of a sudden the cheers appeared.
The crowd was live and in full effect.
How could this be?
I was at a funeral for the old me.
Surrounded by past loves who threw in the towel.
Like they was buying a vowel.
The pallbearers where precious employers talking this and that.
Saying we knew he was finished.
Getting ready to lower casket.
The biggest haters blew a gasket.
Look up in the sky.
Yeah, I said, I knew I can fly.
Raise above the negativity to reach thy destiny.

Marriage

She said I tried... I'm sorry I tried to stay alive...
I didn't mean to let you down.
Then she died.
Who knew that it would end this way?
Left behind are their two adult daughters.
One madly in love.
The other not sure of how to love.
The father. Yes biological. Quite psychological.
Raised them with love and care.
How will he survive the despair?
He will and he won't.
His soul ready to go.
For him nothing else to live for.
His partner and rock is now a body rot.
Rotting back to the essence.
Essence of love.
We arrive out of love only to depart back to the spirit.
So while you are here let your family hear it.
I love you from beginning to end, cuzz forever we will spend...
In the light and love whether here or up above.

The Balance

If we don't try how can we share with the children.
Lessons of how to co-exist with those we admire, but don't truly understand?
I'm not asking you to stop being you.
I'm just asking you to let me in?
I will leave you with this:
The energy you feel when we are together is the source of the universe.
Both positive and negative plus all points in between.
They are dancing in harmony.
One step at a time, until we return to the vibration called the source of creation... come dance with me.

Brady Toliver

Full Moon

Do you remember?
That cold day in December.
When we first met.

Do you remember?
I looked in your eyes.
You damn near cried.

Do you remember?
Your man lied, left you behind.

Do you remember?
You called out of the blue.
I said how do you do?
You asked can I come by?

Do you remember?
I grabbed your hand and slide to your buttocks.

Do you remember?
You said slow down.
A foul for sure.
A baulk I could endure.

Do you remember?
You pulled a rules of engagement
I said what is meant to engage, can never be delayed.

Do you remember?
We pushed upon the glass.
How would this last.

Do you remember?
Etta James playin' in the background.
"At last..." was the beat.
Energy from the floor to the ceiling.
Oh what a feeling.

Do you remember?
We left blind to the thought.
We met in December.
Jan thru March.
Carried the torch.
Flame of our Love.
April thru June.
Our love was in full bloom.
July thru September.
Days of bliss.

Do you remember?
That 1st day of October.
You said you'd be gone til Dec.

Do you remember?
I haven't seen you since

Do you remember?
I got the call that you were gone.
I'm writing this today.
Jan 20.
As I am day dreaming at a coffee shop.
A tap on my shoulder.
I turned around and we locked eyes.
She said have we met?

Don't you remember?
I know it wasn't you.
But that look in her eye.
Let me know you didn't DIE.
Now, I remember!

The Illusion

Picking up the phone.
They say man's main problem is not being able to sit alone in
a room.
Dialing her number.
No response.
No text or email.
Mind starts to go.
IN the land of the NO.
No, not you.
Nobody.
No, not today.
I'm not ready.
No, NO, NO.
Had to catch myself.
Realize what I am dealing with.
She asked.
Why does she Keep attracting the same type of guy?
Well I won't lie.
Karma.
Either how you act, or the "how" in you react to the treatment.
The prognosis of the delinquency.
Oh, but how it can change.
Only when you answer the call of change.
Seem out of your range.
Oh no, your capacity to grow.
Far greater than we KNOW.

The Beat Of Life

Mesmerized by the beat.
This dashing lad.
Knocking 2 da beats.
Funky and unique.
My vision is dashed with heart and soul.

Brady Toliver

Dreams

Doing Remembering Embracing Acknowledged Mental
Stimulation

Dream this world like a lil gurl.
Be this gurl cuzz she will be gone.
Be that boy that enjoys the toys.
Bok Choy is the ingredient.
If the boy is obedient.
Full of greens one may pick up steam.

Remember that time when the bass carried you.
Boom Boom boom.
Yeah, you was up in that room.

That warm embrace of that sweet horn.
Man, it made you thankful Dolly Parton was born.
It was 85 and wanted to rest on her chest.

Acknowledge your life changed when you heard the guitar
chords on Purple Rain.
Hoped those Vanessa Williams pictures was a symbol of what's
to come.
Back and forth is the mental picture that we'd get richer
or wealthy.
Peace of mind is diving.
As if this was just one line.
Cuzz this thing is all one day.

Stimulating the depths of your soul.
One day you will lose control.
Scrambling to find the pieces.
Only to remember that one Dream, were it all is what it seems.

The Come Back

Never knew if I'd make it.
Man, what am I sayin'?
I knew.
Just had to get a new crew.
Cut out the bullshit.
Create my own pull pit.
That old song in my head.
Keeps playin' over and over again.
2 legit, 2 legit 2 Quit.
My pronouns and adjectives make any ad lib suffice.
Who ever knew I'd be fired:
Once,
Twice,
Thrice!
God said ya heard.
Afraid to jump.
She gave me a punch to da balls.
Built up the walls.
No way out, but up.
Hopped in my pick'em up truck.
Grabbed tha rope, boots and water.
Lord imma make it.
So these risks I gotta take!

This is the first book in a 3 book series helping people to release the errors and frustrations of the past. Allowing for a present and future bigger than one can imagine. The next book in this series is "Life's Compass: Who am I, How did I get where I am at, and How do I move forward." A motivational and instructional book about money, education, and finishing the race of life.